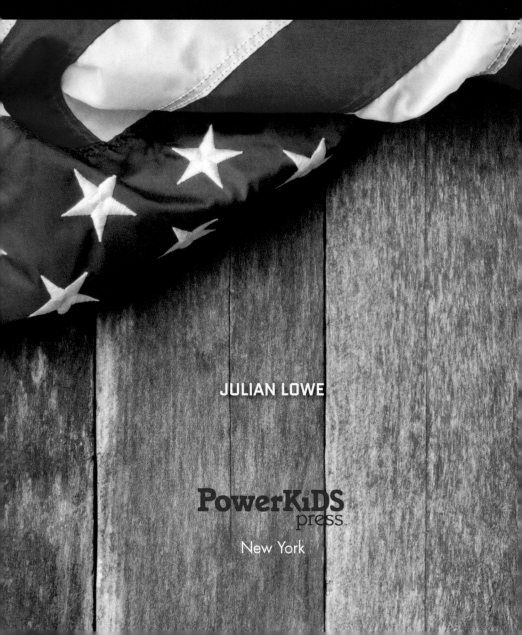

★ ★ ★ ★ ★ ★ **MILITARY FAMILIES** ★ ★ ★ ★ ★ ★

My Aunt Is in the
ARMY RESERVE

JULIAN LOWE

PowerKiDS
press.

New York

Published in 2016 by The Rosen Publishing Group, Inc.
29 East 21st Street, New York, NY 10010

First Edition

Editor: Sarah Machajewski
Book Design: Katelyn Heinle

Photo Credits: Cover, pp. 5, 22 (soldier) Daniel Bendjy/E+/Getty Images; cover backdrop, p. 1 David Smart/Shutterstock.com; pp. 3–4, 6, 8, 10, 12, 14, 16, 18, 20, 22, 24 (camouflage texture) Casper1774/Shutterstock.com; p. 7 (top) kanin.studio/Shutterstock.com; p. 7 (bottom) Monkey Business Images/Shutterstock.com; p. 9 (top) John Moore/Getty Images News/Getty Images; p. 9 (bottom) courtesy of the U.S. Department of Defense; p. 11 Joe Raedle/Getty Images News/Getty Images; pp. 13 (top), 15 (bottom), 19 (top) courtesy of U.S. Army Flickr; p. 13 (bottom) Roy Mehta/Taxi/Getty Images; p. 15 (top) Anchiy/Shutterstock.com; p. 17 StockLite/Shutterstock.com; p. 19 (bottom) Bob Peterson/UpperCut Images/Getty Images; p. 21 Catherine Ledner/Taxi/Getty Images.

Cataloging-in-Publication Data

Lowe, Julian.
My aunt is in the army reserve / by Julian Lowe.
p. cm. — (Military families)
Includes index.
ISBN 978-1-5081-4426-7 (pbk.)
ISBN 978-1-5081-4427-4 (6-pack)
ISBN 978-1-5081-4428-1 (library binding)
1. United States. Army — Reserves — Juvenile literature. 2. United States. Army Reserve — Women — Juvenile literature. I. Lowe, Julian. II. Title.
UA25. L69 2016
355.00973—d23

Manufactured in the United States of America

CONTENTS

Civilian by Day 4

Part of the Military 6

History of the Reserve 8

Signing Up 10

Missing My Aunt 12

Advanced Army Training 14

Jobs for Reserve Soldiers 16

Continued Training 18

What's It Like? 20

My Aunt, My Hero 22

Glossary 23

Index 24

Websites 24

CIVILIAN BY DAY

My aunt is in the Army Reserve. Do you know what that is? The Army Reserve is a part of the U.S. Army. It's made of people who have a **civilian** job, but also have a **role** in the military. My aunt usually works in an office. But sometimes she goes to a special center where she works on her military training. She's even had the chance to work on an **army base**!

My aunt does a lot to **protect** the United States. I'm very proud of her. Thanks to the soldiers in the Army Reserve, our country can stay safe.

MEMBERS OF THE ARMY RESERVE ARE READY TO SERVE OUR COUNTRY WHENEVER THEY'RE NEEDED.

PART OF THE MILITARY

The U.S. military protects and serves the United States and its citizens. Each of the military branches works together to get this job done. The U.S. military has five branches: the army, Marine **Corps**, navy, coast guard, and air force. The Army Reserve is part of the U.S. Army.

The U.S. Army has **active-duty** soldiers. They're the men and women who work for the army full time. The army also has reserve soldiers, such as my aunt. They work for the army part time. My aunt chose to **enlist** in the Army Reserve because it allowed her to keep her regular job while also serving her country.

★ ★ ★
MILITARY MATTERS

The U.S. Army also includes the Army National Guard. It's made of citizen soldiers, or ordinary people who train to be ready when needed.

ACTIVE-DUTY
SOLDIER

ARMY RESERVE
SOLDIER

ACTIVE-DUTY SOLDIERS WORK FOR THE ARMY AS THEIR FULL-TIME JOB. THEY MAY HAVE TO MOVE A LOT OR SERVE OVERSEAS. ARMY RESERVE SOLDIERS CAN STAY IN ONE PLACE AND WORK A REGULAR JOB THAT THEY LOVE.

HISTORY OF THE RESERVE

The Army Reserve was created on April 23, 1908. Congress passed a bill that let the army establish a reserve corps of medical officers. Congress felt this was necessary because there hadn't been enough doctors during the Spanish-American War. By creating the Army Reserve, there was now a group of trained people to call on in times of **crisis**.

The Army Reserve has grown a lot since then. Today, there are more than 200,000 soldiers who specialize in many different fields. My aunt is just one of them! She's proud to be part of a group that has such a long history.

RESERVE MEMBERS ARE CALLED ON IN TIMES OF WAR AND IN TIMES OF CRISIS. IN 2012, THE ARMY ACTIVATED THE ARMY RESERVE TO HELP AFTER SUPERSTORM SANDY. THESE SOLDIERS HELPED GIVE OUT WATER TO PEOPLE IN NEW YORK AND NEW JERSEY WHO WERE AFFECTED BY THE STORM.

SIGNING UP

Like all branches of the military, the Army Reserve has requirements people have to meet before they can sign up. First, they must be a citizen of the United States. Next, they must be between the ages of 17 and 40 to enlist.

Future reserve soldiers must be in good health. They also have to pass an entrance test. Another requirement is having a high school diploma. A diploma is something that shows someone has completed a certain level of schooling. However, the Army Reserve may accept people who have a GED, which is much like a high school diploma.

MANY PEOPLE JOIN THE ARMY RESERVE AFTER FINISHING HIGH SCHOOL. SOME GO ON TO ATTEND COLLEGE. THEY CAN GO TO COLLEGE FULL TIME WHILE ALSO BEING PART OF THE ARMY RESERVE.

★★★ MILITARY MATTERS

A person can enlist in the Army Reserve when they're 17, but they need special permission from their parents.

MISSING MY AUNT

When my aunt enlisted in the Army Reserve, it was a big decision. It was going to change her life! Some people in my family wanted to know what would happen after she signed up. Let me tell you what it was like for us.

After she enlisted, my aunt went to Basic Combat Training (BCT) for 10 weeks. Many people call it "boot camp." I missed my aunt a lot when she was gone. People with family members in the military usually feel this way. It's normal to miss them. It helps to remember that they're away for a very important reason.

★ ★ ★
MILITARY MATTERS
Army Reserve and active-duty soldiers go through the same 10-week BCT.

MY FAMILY WROTE LETTERS TO MY AUNT WHILE SHE WAS AT BASIC TRAINING. SHE WAS ABLE TO WRITE US BACK. SOMETIMES SHE WAS ABLE TO CALL HOME. IT HELPED US FEEL BETTER WHEN WE MISSED HER!

ADVANCED ARMY TRAINING

When my aunt finished basic training, she graduated. My whole family went to her **ceremony**! It was the first time we had seen her in 10 weeks. My aunt wore her army uniform—she was now a soldier in the U.S. Army.

After basic training, my aunt moved on to the next step, which is called Advanced Individual Training (AIT). This training teaches soldiers the skills they need for the job they will have in the army. My aunt went to Signal Corps School. Here, she learned how to work on computers. She works with computers at her civilian job, too.

ARMY RESERVE SOLDIERS CAN USE THE SKILLS THEY LEARN IN THE ARMY TO DO WELL IN THEIR CIVILIAN JOB.

Jobs for Reserve Soldiers

Every soldier has a different reason for joining the Army Reserve. Many people join because the army has a lot of job opportunities. In fact, there are more than 120 kinds of jobs open to reserve soldiers. Soldiers have a chance to train to become accountants, **engineers**, military police, computer specialists, and more.

Just like my aunt, many soldiers pick jobs that help them gain career skills that can be used in the civilian world. My aunt says being in the Army Reserve has taught her problem-solving skills and how to work as part of a team. These skills help her in everyday life.

MANY COMPANIES WANT TO HIRE PEOPLE WHO HAVE A MILITARY BACKGROUND.

CONTINUED TRAINING

Even though my aunt finished basic training and AIT, she still has to keep up with her training. She doesn't work for the army full time, so she trains on the weekends. However, she only has to train for one weekend every month.

Every year, my aunt has to go on something called a Field Training Exercise (FTX) for two weeks. The FTX helps reserve soldiers practice and improve their skills. It prepares them to serve when they're needed. I like that my aunt only has to train once a month. Even though she's part of the army, we can still spend time with her at home!

★ ★ ★
MILITARY MATTERS
A reserve soldier's service usually lasts between three and six years, depending on the job they have.

VIRTUAL COMBAT
TRAINING

MY AUNT HAS TO MAKE SURE SHE'S TRAINED AND READY TO
GO IN CASE THE ARMY NEEDS HER. THE ARMY COULD CALL HER
TO ACTIVE DUTY AT ANY TIME.

What's It Like?

The Army Reserve changed my aunt's life. It changed my family's life, too. We had to say goodbye to my aunt for 10 weeks while she was at training. It was hard because I missed her a lot. But it's okay to feel that way. It means you love and care about someone.

There's one part that's hard about having a family member in the Army Reserve—the army could call on her at any time to help them. That even means she could fight in a war. Sometimes this makes me worried, but talking to my family about it makes me feel better.

ONE OF THE BEST THINGS ABOUT JOINING THE ARMY RESERVE IS THAT SOLDIERS LIVES' DON'T CHANGE MUCH. THIS IS HELPFUL FOR SOLDIERS WITH FAMILIES.

My Aunt, My Hero

It isn't easy to decide to join the military, no matter what branch it is. Men and women have to give up a lot in order to protect our country and the people in it. Because of them, our country is safe.

Servicemen and servicewomen do a lot for our country, but so do their families—just like mine! We have to say goodbye when it's hard and understand the **risks** soldiers face. But it's worth it. My aunt is special in a lot of ways. I'm proud that she's a soldier in the Army Reserve.

GLOSSARY

active duty: Having to do with full-time service in the military. Also, full-time service in the military.

army base: A place owned and operated by the army where soldiers train and equipment is held.

ceremony: A formal occasion that honors an event.

civilian: Having to do with a person not in the armed services or police force.

corps: A group within a branch of a military organization that does a particular kind of work.

crisis: A time of difficulty, trouble, or danger.

engineer: A person who creates, builds, or works on engines, machines, and public works.

enlist: To join.

protect: To keep safe.

risk: A situation in which there is a chance something bad could happen.

role: The part somebody plays in something, such as a job.

INDEX

A
active-duty soldiers,
    6, 7, 12
Advanced Individual
    Training, 14, 18
army base, 4
Army National Guard, 6

B
Basic Combat Training,
    12, 13, 14, 18
boot camp, 12

C
career skills, 16
civilian, 4, 14, 16
crisis, 8

E
enlisting, 6, 10, 11, 12

F
Field Training Exercise, 16

H
history, 8

J
job opportunities, 16

M
military branches, 6,
    10, 22

R
regular job, 4, 6, 7, 14
requirements, 10

U
U.S. Army, 4, 6, 14

W
war, 8, 20
weekend training, 18

WEBSITES

Due to the changing nature of Internet links, PowerKids Press has developed an online list of websites related to the subject of this book. This site is updated regularly. Please use this link to access the list: www.powerkidslinks.com/mili/aunt